SEXUAL INTEGRITY

A Sexual Revolution Called Purity

SEXUAL INTEGRITY

A Sexual Revolution Called Purity

MAJORING IN MEN®

The Curriculum for Men

by

Edwin Louis Cole

RESOLUTE BOOKS

Southlake, Texas

Unless otherwise indicated, all Scripture quotations are taken from the King James Version of the Holy Bible. Scripture quotations marked (NIV) are taken from the *Holy Bible, New International Version*®, NIV®, © 1973, 1978, 1984 by the International Bible Society. Used by permission of Zondervan. All rights reserved. Scripture quotations marked (AMP) are taken from the *Amplified® Bible*, © 1954, 1958, 1962, 1964, 1965, 1987 by The Lockman Foundation. Used by permission. (www.Lockman.org). Scripture quotations marked (TLB) are taken from The Living Bible, © 1971. Used by permission of Tyndale House Publishers, Inc., Wheaton, Illinois 60189. All rights reserved.

SEXUAL INTEGRITY WORKBOOK:
A Sexual Revolution Called Purity

Christian Men's Network
P.O. Box 93478
Southlake, TX 76092
www.ChristianMensNetwork.com

Facebook.com/EdwinLouisCole

ISBN: 978-1-93862-914-3
Printed in the United States of America

Published by:
Resolute Books™
1030 Hunt Valley Circle
New Kensington, PA 15068

4 5 6 7 8 9 10 11 / 20 19 18

TABLE OF CONTENTS

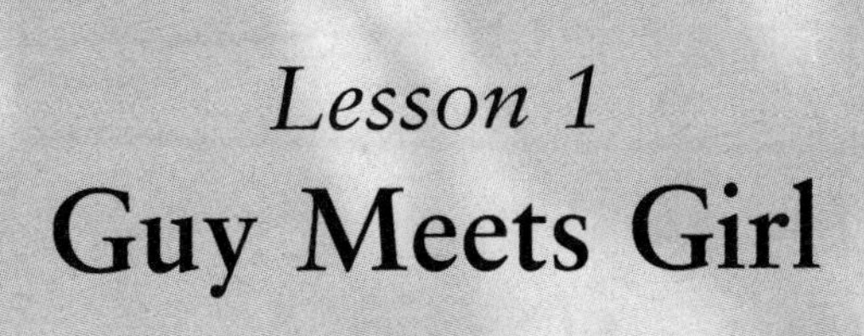

Lesson 1
Guy Meets Girl

Lesson 1

Guy Meets Girl

A. Every man has _________ thing he can give only _________ time to _________ woman in _________ lifetime. It is ______________________________________. *(pages 21-22)*

B. Decisions translate into: *(circle one) (page 26)*

a. work   b. energy   c. emotion

1. Once the choice is made, you must continue to make it: *(circle one) (page 26)*

   a. daily   b. weekly   c. when you're in church

2. Integrity can be defined as "soundness," "being complete or undivided" or "firm adherence to a code." **In your own words**, how would you define "sexual integrity"?

   ____

   ____

   ____

For Further Study:

Decisions – *"Do you not know that if you continually surrender yourselves to anyone to do his will, you are the slaves of him whom you obey, whether that be to sin, which leads to death, or to obedience which leads to righteousness (right doing and right standing with God)?"* Romans 6:16 AMP.
Integrity – *"The integrity of the upright shall guide them"* Proverbs 11:3; *"Whoever heard me spoke well of me, and those who saw me commended me ... I put on righteousness as my clothing; justice was my robe and my turban ... I made a covenant with my eyes not to look lustfully at a girl"* Job 29:11, 14; 31:1 NIV.
Choose wisely – *"Every prudent man acts out of knowledge, but a fool exposes his folly"* Proverbs 13:16 NIV.

C. Read: *"For God wants you to be holy and pure, and to keep clear of all sexual sin so that each of you will marry in holiness and honor—not in lustful passion as the heathen do, in their ignorance of God and his ways"* 1 Thessalonians 4:3, 5 TLB.

What do these verses mean to you about sexuality?

____

____

____

D. People were created to be the same. *(page 27)*

___ True ___ False

1. Name a similarity people share. *(pages 27-28)*

   ____

2. Men and women were created to be different. *(page 28)*

   ___ True ___ False

3. What are men more motivated by? *(page 28)* ____________________

For Further Study:

Each person is uniquely created by God – Psalm 139:13; Jeremiah 1:5.
God wants us to be holy and pure – Ephesians 5:15-17; Titus 2:12-14.
Everything God made is good – Genesis 1:31; Psalm 139:15.
One similarity that all people share is the will to choose – Galatians 5:16-25.
Obedience – *"If ye be willing and obedient, ye shall eat the good of the land"* Isaiah 1:19; *"But if anyone keeps looking steadily into God's law for free men, he will not only remember it but he will do what it says, and God will greatly bless him in everything he does"* James 1:25 TLB.
God's power is released to the degree that obedience is exercised – Revelation 2:26.

4. What are women more motivated by? *(page 28)* ____________________

E. What are the "three most powerful words in the world"? *(pages 28-29)*

____

1. Read: *"Pretty words may hide a wicked heart, just as a pretty glaze covers a common clay pot"* Proverbs 26:23 TLB.

   Read: *"Having a form of godliness but denying its power ... They are the kind who worm their way into homes and gain control over weak-willed women"* 2 Timothy 3:5-6 NIV.

   This is a warning about women being deceived by what? *(page 29)*

   ____

For Further Study:

John 3:16 – This is God saying to mankind, *"I love you."* It is the foundation upon which God has created all things.
Most of what is called love today is really lust – 1 John 2:15, 16.
Love and sex – *"Love does not demand its own way"* 1 Corinthians 13:5 TLB.
Women beware deceitful men – *"They are good speakers, and simple-minded people are often fooled by them"* Romans 16:18 TLB; *"For such persons do not serve our Lord Christ but their own appetites and base desires, and by ingratiating and flattering speech, they beguile the hearts of the unsuspecting and simpleminded [people]"* Romans 16:18 AMP; *"Detestable, disobedient and unfit for doing anything good"* Titus 1:16 NIV; *"A malicious man disguises himself with his lips, but in his heart he harbors deceit. Though his speech is charming, do not believe him, for seven abominations fill his heart"* Proverbs 26:24, 25 NIV.

2. Read: *"Do not lust in your heart after her beauty or let her captivate you with her eyes, for the prostitute reduces you to a loaf of bread, and the adulteress preys upon your very life"* Proverbs 6:25-26 NIV.

   This is a warning about men being deceived by what? *(page 29)*

   ____

F. Men and women are to ________________________________ each other. *(circle one) (page 29)*

   a. compete with b. nag c. complement

1. Being ______________ can be a blessing, but being ___________________ never is. *(pages 29-30)*

For Further Study:

Men beware – *"All at once he followed her like an ox going to the slaughter ... little knowing it will cost him his life"* Proverbs 7:22-23 NIV; *"I find more bitter than death the woman who is a snare, whose heart is a trap and whose hands are chains. The man who pleases God will escape her, but the sinner she will ensnare"* Ecclesiastes 7:26 NIV; Proverbs 2:16-19; 5:3-5.
Lust is degenerative – 2 Samuel 13:1, 13, 15; James 1:14, 15; *"But the wicked are like the troubled sea, when it cannot rest, whose waters cast up mire and dirt"* Isaiah 57:20; *"The way of transgressors is hard"* Proverbs 13:15.
God had a plan for men and women – Matthew 19:4-6; Mark 10:6-9; Ephesians 5:31.

2. Read: *"So God created man in his own image, in the image of God created he him; male and female created he them ... And the LORD God said, It is not good that the man should be alone; I will make him an help meet for him"* Genesis 1:27; 2:18.

   If God had created a woman from anything other than what was already in Adam, He would have

   created an ______________________________ being. *(page 30)*

3. God has in Him both the feminine and the masculine. *(page 31)*

   ___ True ___ False

4. Name some qualities and characteristics unique to women. *(pages 30-31)*

   ____

5. Name some qualities and characteristics unique to men. *(pages 30-31)*

   ____

For Further Study:

"So God created man in his own image, in the image of God created he him; male and female created he them" Genesis 1:27.

God reveals the equality in the creation of man and woman – Genesis 2:23; Ephesians 5:28-29.

The rib is symbolic of characteristics God took to make the woman's nature – *"She shall be called Woman, because she was taken out of Man"* Genesis 2:23; *"For as the woman is from the man, even so is the man also by the woman; but all things of God"* 1 Corinthians 11:12.

6. Read: *"Therefore shall a man leave his father and his mother, and shall cleave unto his wife: and they shall be one flesh"* Genesis 2:24.

   When man and woman come together in marriage, they are united as ______________________

   _______________. *(page 31)*

Practical:

1. Decisions convert into energy. Your decision to remain pure before God will become energy that propels you. Write out your decision here.

   ____

   ____

   ____

For Further Study:

Romans 6:16 – You are the slave of whoever you surrender yourself to.
"While they promise them liberty, they themselves are the servants of corruption: for of whom a man is overcome, of the same is he brought in bondage" 2 Peter 2:19.
The double-minded waver between right and wrong because they are undecided – 1 Kings 18:21.
They profess to hate sin, but they have a lingering love for it – James 4:1.
They do not have a right understanding of good and evil – Hebrews 5:14.

2. Men and women are tempted in similar ways but, in general, are motivated differently. In what ways are you tempted? What motivates you? How can you create a "pure" environment where you are not tempted or motivated in the wrong way?

Problem Area	How to Avoid It
______________________	______________________
______________________	______________________
______________________	______________________

Repeat this prayer out loud:

Father, please forgive me for ignorance concerning my sexual integrity. I choose to keep myself pure from sexual immorality. I choose to be honorable with my words, especially not to manipulate women or deceive them or myself into thinking I'm doing them a service when I'm really just gratifying my lusts. Help me become a pillar of strength and moral uprightness for all the world to see. In Jesus' Name, I ask, Amen.

Principles I want to memorize:

Self Test *Lesson 1*

1. What are the "three most powerful words in the world"?

    ____

2. Write down two major differences between men and women, other than physical characteristics.

    ____

    ____

3. The differences between men and women are always going to create problems.

    ___ True ___ False

4. Being lonely is never a blessing.

    ___ True ___ False

5. God has in Him both the feminine and the masculine.

    ___ True ___ False

6. God created Eve from the dust of the earth.

    ___ True ___ False

Keep this test for your own records.

Lesson 2

The Sign of the Covenant

Lesson 2

The Sign of the Covenant

A. Reports show that most people learn about sex: *(circle one) (pages 33-34)*

a. at church b. at school c. at home d. on their own

1. Read: *"[The] Priests' lips should flow with the knowledge of God so the people will learn God's laws. The priests are the messengers of the Lord of Hosts, and men should come to them for guidance"* Malachi 2:7 TLB.

2. According to this verse, where is one Biblical place people can learn about sex? *(page 34)*

   ____

B. Sex is the sign of the ____. *(page 35)*

For Further Study:

Hebrews, chapters 9 through 13, speaks of the Old Testament blood covenant and of the New Testament blood covenant.

"And almost all things are by the law purged with blood; and without shedding of blood is no remission" Hebrews 9:22.

"For the law having a shadow of good things to come ... can never with those sacrifices which they offered year by year continually make the comers thereunto perfect ... He taketh away the first, that he may establish the second. By the which will we are sanctified through the offering of the body of Jesus Christ once for all" Hebrews 10:1, 9-10.

1. The covenant considered most sacred in human history is: *(circle one) (page 35)*

   a. blood b. faith c. spirit d. vow

2. Read: *"This is my covenant, which ye shall keep, between me and you and thy seed after thee; Every man child among you shall be circumcised. And ye shall circumcise the flesh of your foreskin; and it shall be a token of the covenant betwixt me and you"* Genesis 17:10-11.

For Further Study:

"I will put my laws into their hearts, and in their minds will I write them; And their sins and iniquities will I remember no more. Now where remission of these is, there is no more offering for sin ... Let us draw near with a true heart in full assurance of faith, having our hearts sprinkled from an evil conscience, and our bodies washed with pure water" Hebrews 10:16-18, 22.

"Marriage is honourable in all, and the bed undefiled: but whoremongers and adulterers God will judge" Hebrews 13:4.

"Wherefore Jesus also, that he might sanctify the people with his own blood, suffered without the gate ... By him therefore let us offer the sacrifice of praise to God continually, that is, the fruit of our lips giving thanks to his name. But to do good and to communicate forget not: for with such sacrifices God is well pleased" Hebrews 13:12, 15-16.

"We have a good conscience, in all things willing to live honestly" Hebrews 13:18.

3. Write the correct letter in the blank that completes the sentence. *(pages 37-40)*

___ The sign of the Abrahamic covenant is	a. identification
___ As an outward sign of the covenant, God changed Abraham's	b. uncleanness
___ Circumcision represents cutting away	c. circumcision
___ For covenant to be meaningful, it must start in our	d. baptism
___ Shedding of blood brings forgiveness of	e. marriage
___ The New Testament sign of the covenant is	f. heart
___ Baptism is an act of	g. name
___ Circumcision and baptism are external evidences of an internal	h. work
___ Sex is the sign of the covenant of	i. sin

C. Sex, baptism and circumcision are all external ______________________ of an internal ______________________. *(page 40)*

For Further Study:

"Then God said to Abraham, 'As for you, you must keep my covenant, you and your descendants after you for the generations to come. This is my covenant with you and your descendants after you, the covenant you are to keep: Every male among you shall be circumcised. You are to undergo circumcision, and it will be the sign of the covenant between me and you'" Genesis 17:9-11 NIV.

D. Fill in the blanks on the following chart, from the chart on page 41 of your book.

Holy Covenant	**Internal Work**	**External Work**
Abraham	____________________	____________________
	____________________	____________________

Result: Righteousness from entering a blood covenant, bringing glory to God

Jesus	____________________	____________________
	____________________	____________________

Result: Righteousness from entering a blood covenant, bringing glory to God

Marriage	____________________	____________________
	____________________	____________________

Result: Righteousness from entering a blood covenant, bringing glory to God

For Further Study:

Christ gave His blood for our *"eternal redemption"* and is *"the mediator of a new covenant"* Hebrews 9:12, 15 NIV. *"For this reason a man will leave his father and mother and be united to his wife, and the two will become one flesh"* Ephesians 5:31NIV; Genesis 2:24; Matthew 19:5, 6.

E. Living together is ______________________________. Getting married is

______________________________. *(page 42)*

1. The shedding of blood in the first sexual intimacy is symbolic of a blood covenant. *(page 42)*

   ___ True ___ False

2. Marriage is ______________________. It is a ______________________. *(page 43)*

3. Keeping sex pure within marriage is what it means to have ______________________

   ____. *(page 43)*

For Further Study:

"The husband should fulfill his marital duty to his wife, and likewise the wife to her husband" 1 Corinthians 7:3 NIV.
"Husbands, in the same way be considerate as you live with your wives, and treat them with respect as the weaker partner and as heirs with you of the gracious gift of life, so that nothing will hinder your prayers" 1 Peter 3:7.
"And you husbands must be loving and kind to your wives" Colossians 3:19 TLB.
How husbands and wives are to relate – Ephesians 5:25-33

Practical:

1. Read: *"And so, dear brothers, I plead with you to give your bodies to God. Let them be a living sacrifice, holy—the kind he can accept. When you think of what he has done for you, is this too much to ask?"* Romans 12:1 TLB.

   In light of what we are studying, what does this verse say to you personally about your body?

   ____

   ____

   ____

For Further Study:

Jesus affirms the sacredness of marriage – *"For this reason a man will leave his father and mother and be united to his wife, and the two will become one flesh. So they are no longer two, but one. Therefore what God has joined together, let man not separate"* Mark 10:7 NIV.

Integrity – Firm adherence to a code of especially moral values; Incorruptibility (dictionary definition)

"I beg you ... to live and act in a way worthy of those who have been chosen for such wonderful blessings as these" Ephesians 4:1 TLB.

"Dear friends, I urge you ... to abstain from sinful desires, which war against your soul" 1 Peter 2:11 NIV.

2. How do people where you live enter into covenants today? Are covenants kept or broken?

____

____

____

Repeat this prayer out loud:

Father, I think I finally understand. I admit my errors of the past and thank You for helping me see the awesome covenant You have provided for me in marriage. I want to follow that covenant and not break it with my eyes, my thoughts or my body. I ask You to help me keep my covenant with You, and I thank You in advance because I know You are guiding and leading me. In Jesus' Name, I pray. Amen.

Principles I want to memorize:

Self Test *Lesson 2*

1. Church is simply not the place where sex should be taught.

   ___ True ___ False

2. In human history, blood covenants are the highest covenant that can be made between people.

   ___ True ___ False

3. What was the sign of the Abrahamic covenant? *(circle one)*

   a. faith

   b. works

   c. circumcision

4. The covenants God gave are an external ______________________________ of an

   ____.

5. Name three signs of covenant in marriage which follow an internal work of the heart.

   a. ______________________________________

   b. ______________________________________

   c. ______________________________________

6. Do all of God's covenants bring Him glory?

   ___ Yes ___ No

7. What is the sacred sign of the covenant of marriage? ____

8. Living together is involvement. Getting married is a ____.

Keep this test for your own records.

Lesson 3

Sex Before Marriage

Lesson 3
Sex Before Marriage

A. Lust is the ______________________ of the ________________ God created. *(page 45)*

1. Lust desires to benefit ________________ at the expense of ________________. *(page 46)*

   Love desires to benefit ________________ at the expense of ________________. *(page 46)*

2. God made sex for ____________________ and ______________________, not for ________________________ and __________________________. *(page 46)*

3. God is a creator. Satan is a ________________________. *(page 46)*

4. Satan made sex to entrap people in sin. *(page 46)*

   ___ True ___ False

5. God made sex good. Man, under Satan's influence, makes it bad. *(page 46)*

   ___ True ___ False

6. God creates the positive, builds on a positive and always ___________ on a positive. *(page 46)*

For Further Study:

Satan counterfeits – 2 Thessalonians. 2:9, 10; *"And no marvel; for Satan himself is transformed into an angel of light"* 2 Corinthians 11:14. Love, not lust, satisfies – *"The Lord thy God in the midst of thee is mighty … he will rest in his love"* Zephaniah 3:17; *"From whence come wars and fightings among you? come they not hence, even of your lusts that war in your members?"* James 4:1, 2. Lust is degenerative – James 1:14, 15. *"But the wicked are like the troubled sea, when it cannot rest, whose waters cast up mire and dirt"* Isaiah 57:20; *"The way of transgressors is hard"* Proverbs 13:15; 2 Samuel 13:1, 13, 15.
Love and sex – *"Love does not demand its own way"* 1 Corinthians 13:5 TLB.

7. Name some effects of lust. *(page 46)*

   a. ________________

   b. ________________

   c. ________________

8. Name some benefits of love. *(page 46)*

   a. ________________

   b. ________________

   c. ________________

   d. ________________

9. Abortion is a blood ________________ to the god of ________________. *(page 47)*

For Further Study:

"Then when lust hath conceived, it bringeth forth sin: and sin, when it is finished, bringeth forth death" James 1:15. Lust limits; love releases – *"The words of the Lord Jesus, how he said, It is more blessed to give than to receive"* Acts 20:35; John 10:10; 15:13; Romans 12:9, 10; 1 Corinthians 13:4-7; Ephesians 5:25; 2 Timothy 3:2; Hebrews 13:4; James 4:1-3; 1 Peter 4:8-10. *"Love endures long and is patient and kind; love never is envious nor boils over with jealousy, is not boastful or vainglorious, does not display itself haughtily. It is not conceited (arrogant and inflated with pride); it is not rude (unmannerly) and does not act unbecomingly. Love (God's love in us) does not insist on its own rights or its own way, for it is not self-seeking; it is not touchy or fretful or resentful; it takes no account of the evil done to it [it pays no attention to a suffered wrong]"* 1 Corinthians 13:4, 5 AMP.

B. Look up 1 Corinthians 6:18 KJV. *"Flee* ____________________________________. *Every sin that a man doeth is without the body; but he that committeth* ____________________________ *sinneth against his own* ______________________*."*

What is a definition of fornication? *(page 47)*

____

For Further Study:

God's prohibition of sex outside marriage was given to protect sex. *"Marriage is honorable in all, and the bed undefiled"* Hebrews 13:4.
The woman should be the glory of the man, not the object of his lust and the cause of his separation from God – 1 Corinthians 11:7.
God's Word is filled with warnings to young men concerning their unbridled passions – Proverbs 7:24, 25. *"Flee fornication ... he that committeth fornication sinneth against his own body"* 1 Corinthians 6:18-20.
Sex Sins – *"But fornication, and all uncleanness, or covetousness, let it not be once named among you, as becometh saints"* Ephesians 5:3; Psalm 101:2-8; Romans 6; Galatians 5:16-24; *"It is God's will that you should be sanctified: that you should avoid sexual immortality; that each of you should learn to control his own body in a way that is holy and honorable, not is passionate lust like the heathen, who do not know God"* 1 Thessalonians 4:3-5 NIV; Ephesians 4:17-19; 5:15-17; 1 Timothy 3:15; Titus 2:12-14; 1 John 2:3-6; 5:18; 3 John 11.

C. Old Testament rules about virginity:

1. If a man ______________________ a woman's virginity, he was to ________________________
   ____________________________. (page 47)

2. If a woman _________________________________ her virginity outside of marriage, she was to
   ______________________________________. (page 47)

3. Read Deuteronomy 22:17-27.

   Is there a doubt as to whether or not God wants both the man and the woman to be virgins at marriage?

   ___ Yes ___ No

For Further Study:

"And if a man entice a maid that is not betrothed, and lie with her, he shall surely endow her to be his wife. If her father utterly refuse to give her unto him, he shall pay money according to the dowry of virgins" Exodus 22:16, 17. *"If a man find a damsel that is a virgin, which is not betrothed, and lay hold on her, and lie with her, and they be found; Then the man that lay with her shall give unto the damsel's father fifty shekels of silver, and she shall be his wife; because he hath humbled her, he may not put her away all his days"* Deuteronomy 22:28, 29.

D. The punishment for losing virginity was severe so the ______________________________ ______________________________ would come upon Israel and they would get rid of ________________, including ____. *(page 50)*

1. Read: "*The fear of the Lord is the beginning of knowledge; Fools despise wisdom and instruction*" Proverbs 1:7.

   Read: "*And by the reverent, worshipful fear of the Lord men depart from and avoid evil*" Proverbs 16:6b AMP.

2. Why is it a benefit to "fear the Lord"? *(page 50)*

   ____

For Further Study:

The fear of the Lord – "*The fear of the Lord is the beginning of wisdom*" Proverbs 9:10; "*By the fear of the Lord men depart from evil*" Proverbs16:6; "*Then had the churches rest throughout all Judaea and Galilee and Samaria, and were edified; and walking in the fear of the Lord, and in the comfort of the Holy Ghost, were multiplied*" Acts 9:31; John 16:8.
Conviction of sin within the Church – "*But the face of the Lord is against them that do evil*" 1 Peter 3:12; "*Righteousness exalteth a nation: but sin is a reproach to any people*" Proverbs 14:34; "*Ye are the light of the world. A city that is set on a hill cannot be hid*" Matthew 5:14; "*If therefore the light that is in thee be darkness, how great is that darkness*" Matthew 6:23; "*By the blessing of the upright the city is exalted: but it is overthrown by the mouth of the wicked*" Proverbs 11:11.
God commanded Israel to rid itself of all sexual sins – Deuteronomy 22:22-24.

E. Men are responsible for ______________________________ about women. *(page 51)*

A man who slanders a woman is subject to the ______________________________

______________________________. *(page 51)*

F. Define "lasciviousness." *(page 53)*

____

G. The standards of the Bible change with each generation. *(page 54)*

___ True ___ False

1. We cannot take portions of the Bible to justify our ______________________________. *(page 54)*
2. We must take our ____________________ and make them conform to ____________________

   ____________________. *(page 54)*

For Further Study:

Deuteronomy 22:13-19 – This passage of Scripture addresses the slandering of women.
"Lascivious" means "wantonness, lustful, lewd, unrestrained." See Galatians 5:19; Ephesians 4:19; 1 Peter 4:3; Jude 4.
Using the Word of God to justify a sinful lifestyle is wrong. Deuteronomy 4:2; 12:32; Revelation 22:18-19; *"Wherefore lay apart all filthiness and superfluity of naughtiness, and receive with meekness the engrafted word, which is able to save your soul. But be ye doers of the word, and not hearers only, deceiving your own selves"* James 1:21-22.
"All scripture is given by inspiration of God, and is profitable for doctrine, for reproof, for correction, for instruction in righteousness: That the man of God may be perfect, thoroughly furnished unto all good works" 2 Timothy 3:16-17.

H. By your relationship to God, you ______________________________ what happens all around you. Every man who renounces sin grows in ______________________ and ______________________ and makes an ______________________ on the world around him. *(pages 58-59)*

To the degree that a nation loses its ______________________________, it will lose its influence in the world. *(page 59)*

Practical:

1. In what practical way can you flee fornication?

   ____

2. Is God very serious about you keeping yourself sexually pure?

   ____

For Further Study:

"Know ye not, that to whom ye yield yourselves servants to obey, his servants ye are to whom ye obey; whether of sin unto death, or of obedience unto righteousness? But God be thanked, that ye were the servants of sin, but ye have obeyed from the heart that form of doctrine which was delivered you. Being then made free from sin, ye became the servants of righteousness" Romans 6:16-18.

Deuteronomy 28 outlines the conditions for a nation to receive either the blessings or the curses of God. God does not intend for His children to live under a curse.

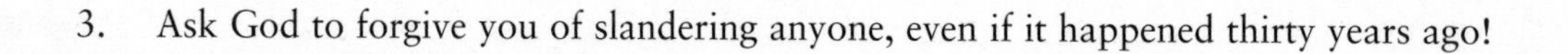

3. Ask God to forgive you of slandering anyone, even if it happened thirty years ago!

Repeat this prayer out loud:

Father, in Jesus' Name, thank You for showing me the seriousness of sexual purity. Give me the wisdom to walk in Your way, and guard my heart and life from sin. Please help me find friends who revere and worship You. Amen.

Principles I want to memorize:

Self Test *Lesson 3*

1. Love always desires to benefit ______________________ at the expense of ______________________.

   Lust desires to benefit ______________________ at the expense of ______________________.

2. The Bible talks about men receiving a curse for gossiping and lying about a woman.

   ___ True ___ False

3. "Lasciviousness" can be defined as "loosed-from-restraint ______________________."

4. Name some of the problems that arise due to sexual relationships outside of marriage.

   a. ______________________

   b. ______________________

   c. ______________________

5. The comfort of the Holy Ghost is balanced by the ______________________.

6. **In your own words,** write what it means to "fear God."

   ____

   ____

   ____

7. You alone are responsible for yourself. Therefore, your life has no effect on this world.

   ___ True ___ False

Keep this test for your own records.

Lesson 4

Pornography, Masturbation and Lust

Lesson 4

Pornography, Masturbation and Lust

A. Lustful thoughts that rise up within you might actually come from ______________________________

______________________________. *(pages 61-62)*

1. Pornography is specifically designed to ______________________________

   ______________________________. *(page 63)*

2. Read: *"Beloved, I implore you as aliens and strangers and exiles [in this world] to abstain from the sensual urges (the evil desires, the passions of the flesh, your lower nature) that wage war against the soul"* 1 Peter 2:11 AMP.

   Read: *"I made a covenant with my eyes not to look with lust upon a girl"* Job 31:1 TLB.

   Read: *"So whoever cleanses himself [from what is ignoble and unclean, who separates himself from contact with contaminating and corrupting influences] will [then himself] be a vessel set apart and useful for honorable and noble purposes, consecrated and profitable to the Master, fit and ready for any good work"* 2 Timothy 2:21 AMP.

For Further Study:

1 Peter 4:3-6 tells us to separate ourselves from the things of the flesh.
Proverbs 6:24-35 and Matthew 5:28 warn against lust and the results of giving in to lusts.
"But thou, O man of God, flee these things; and follow after righteousness, godliness, faith, love, patience, meekness. Fight the good fight of faith, lay hold on eternal life, whereunto thou art also called, and hast professed a good profession before many witnesses" 1 Timothy 6:11-12.

B. An image in the mind actually becomes an ______________________. *(page 63)*

1. Pornography and masturbation are problems only for single people. *(page 64)*

   ___ True ___ False

2. All sin promises to ______________________ and ______________________, but desires only to ______________________ and ______________________. *(page 64)*

3. Name three things pornography does to a person. *(page 65)*

   a. ______________________

   b. ______________________

   c. ______________________

For Further Study:

A person cannot engage in pornography without being affected by the unclean spirits which produced it – Proverbs 6:27-28.

Pornography becomes an act of idolatry. The image is created in the mind of the viewer – Ezekiel 8:12. In turn, pornography creates a stronghold in the mind and a snare to the life – Psalm 106:36.

Idolatrous fantasizing and private sex sins are a sin against one's own manhood – Deuteronomy 7:26.

Sin's deception – sin promises to serve but creates bondage instead. *"Jesus answered them, Verily, verily, I say unto you, Whosoever committeth sin is the servant of sin"* John 8:34. Also, see 2 Peter 2:19.

4. Name some effects of pornography. *(page 66)*

   a. ______________________________

   b. ______________________________

   c. ______________________________

   d. ______________________________

C. What many look for through pornography is ______________________________. *(page 66)*

   1. Instead of closeness, pornography produces ______________________________. *(page 66)*

   2. Pornography is a counterfeit for ______________________________. *(page 69)*

For Further Study:

Love, not lust, satisfies – *"The Lord thy God in the midst of thee is mighty … he will rest in his love"* Zephaniah 3:17. *"From whence come wars and fightings among you? Come they not hence, even of your lusts that war in your members?"* James 4:1, 2.
Lust is degenerative – James 1:14, 15; *"But the wicked are like the troubled sea, when it cannot rest, whose waters cast up mire and dirt"* Isaiah 57:20; *"The way of the transgressor is hard"* Proverbs 13:15; 2 Samuel 13:1, 13, 15.
Love and sex – *"Love does not demand its own way"* 1 Corinthians13:5 TLB.
Sin alters behavior – *"When the woman saw that the tree was good for food … she took of the fruit thereof, and did eat, and gave also unto her husband … and he did eat. And the eyes of them both were opened, and they knew that they were naked; and they sewed fig leaves together, and made themselves aprons. And they heard the voice of the Lord God walking in the garden … and Adam and his wife hid themselves from the presence of the Lord"* Genesis 3:6-8.

3. Prayer alone can produce ____. *(page 69)*

4. The greatest intimacy a man and woman will know will come out of times of ________________ ________________________________. *(page 69)*

For Further Study:

Prayer produces intimacy – Example: *"They joined with the other believers in regular attendance at … prayer meetings … And all the believers … shared everything with each other"* Acts 2:42-44 TLB.
God's desire for intimacy – John 17:21; *"But as many as received him, to them gave he power to become the sons of God, even to them that believe on his name"* John 1:12.
Christ's provisions mirror ours – *"Love your wives, even as Christ also loved the church"* Ephesians 5:25.
Everything God made is good – Genesis 1:31; Psalm 139:15.
Man makes good things negative – Genesis 3:17.
Lust is insatiable, love is easily satisfied – Ecclesiastes 5:10; 1 Corinthians 13:4; James 4:1.

D. Write the correct letter in the blank for the word that completes the sentence. *(page 70)*

___ God created the earth in the ______________________.	a. satisfying
___ Man, through sin, has recreated the earth in the ______________________.	b. negative
___ Love is ______________________,	c. obedient
___ but lust is ______________________.	d. power
___ God's ______________________ is released in your life	e. unconditional
___ to the degree that you are ______________________.	f. positive
___ God's promises are ______________________,	g. insatiable
___ but His love is ______________________.	h. conditional

For Further Study:

Obedience – *"If ye be willing and obedient, ye shall eat the good of the land"* Isaiah 1:19; James 1:25 TLB.
God's power is released to the degree that obedience is exercised – Revelation 2:26.
Lust limits; love releases – *"The words of the Lord Jesus, how he said, It is more blessed to give than to receive"* Acts 20:35; John 10:10; 15:13; Romans 12:9, 10; 1 Corinthians 13:4-7; Ephesians 5:25; 2 Timothy 3:2; Hebrews 13:4; James 4:1-3; 1 Peter 4:8-10.

E. Fill in the blanks from the chart on page 71.

KINGDOM OF ________	**KINGDOM OF SATAN**
POSITIVE	______________________
__________ is Lord.	Self is ____________________.
Love	______________________
	Lust - morally
____________	Perversion
	______________________
	Adultery
Prayer	______________________
____________	Distance
	______________________
Blessing	______________________

For Further Study:

The characteristics of the kingdom emanate from the character of the king – Hosea 4:9.
Satan counterfeits – 2 Thessalonians 2:9, 10; *"And no marvel; for Satan himself is translated into an angel of light"* 2 Corinthians 11:14.
God has good purposes for sex – Genesis 1:27, 28, 31; Malachi 2:15; Matthew 19:4, 5.
The world has perverted sex – Romans 1:24; The Church must correct the perversion – Malachi 2:7.
Sex is honorable – Hebrews 13:4; *"Every good gift and every perfect gift is from above, and cometh down from the Father of lights, with whom is no variableness, neither shadow of turning"* James 1:17.

F. When you do ____________________________, God will do ____________________________. *(page 71)*

1. You can program your conscious mind with ____. *(pages 71-72)*

2. Renew your __________________________________ daily. *(page 72)*

3. You're never too _______________________ or too ______________________ to start. *(page 72)*

Practical:

1. A married man makes conversation with a single woman at work and eventually they find themselves in a car kissing. Has he sinned? ____________

   An unmarried man and woman engage in oral sex but don't lose their blood covenant through intercourse. Is God pleased with them? ____________

For Further Study:

God's love is unconditional; His promises are conditional. *"If ye be willing and obedient, ye shall eat the good of the land"* Isaiah 1:19; Hebrews 11:6; James 1:25.

Example: Promise to David – 2 Samuel 7:8; Fight to obtain it – Hebrews 11:32-33; David's strategy for victory – 2 Samuel 5:22-25

"This book of the law shall not depart out of thy mouth; but thou shalt meditate therein day and night, that thou mayest observe to do according to all that is written therein: for then thou shalt make thy way prosperous, and then thou shalt have good success" Joshua 1:8. Also, see Psalm 119:97; Jeremiah 31:33; Acts 17:11; Hebrews 8:10.

2. What is in your environment that feeds lust? What action can you take to lessen the influence?

___

___

3. Read Romans 7:23 and comment on how it applies to your life.

___

___

Repeat this prayer out loud:

Father, in Jesus' Name, I make a covenant with my eyes not to look at what is evil and unclean. I will give my attention only to those things that glorify You. Thank You, Father, for keeping me pure and helping me to flee from evil. Amen.

For Further Study:

Renew your mind – *"Lie not … seeing that ye have put off the old man … And have put on the new man"* Colossians 3:9-10; *"And be not conformed to this world: but be ye transformed by the renewing of your mind, that ye may prove what is that good, and acceptable, and perfect, will of God"* Romans 12:2. Also, see Ephesians 4:23; Philippians 2:5.

Self Test *Lesson 4*

1. Name some of the results of pornography in a man's life.

   a. ______________________________

   b. ______________________________

   c. ______________________________

2. In what way is pornography a counterfeit for prayer?

   ____

   ____

3. All sin: *(circle one)*

   a. promises to please and serve

   b. enslaves and dominates

   c. changes behavior

   d. all of the above

4. All of God's promises are unconditional. God's love is conditional.

   ___ True ___ False

5. The habit of masturbation becomes an act of worshipping an idol.

   ___ True ___ False

6. Many men and women look for intimacy in pornography. Instead of producing closeness, pornography produces: *(circle one)*

   a. madness b. distance c. release

Keep this test for your own records.

Lesson 5

Freedom from the Effects of Abuse & Receiving the Glory of Virginity

Lesson 5

Freedom from the Effects of Abuse & Receiving the Glory of Virginity

I. Freedom from the Effects of Abuse (Chapter 5)

A. Past abuse becomes a stumbling block in relationships and ruins the ability to experience

______________________________. *(page 74)*

B. The principle of release is found in what verses of Scripture? *(page 77)*

____

1. You ____________________ what you do not ____________________. *(page 78)*

2. To forgive as God forgives, it must be done in the power of

______________________________. *(page 78)*

3. Negative sexual experiences fade away with time. *(page 79)* ___ True ___ False

---

For Further Study:

The principle of release, John 20:22, 23, states that people are free to become what God wants them to be only after sins are released – Matthew 6:14-15.

"*[Now having received the Holy Spirit and being led and directed by Him] if you forgive the sins of anyone, they are forgiven; if you retain the sins of anyone, they are retained*" John 20:23 AMP.

When you forgive, release – John 20:22; 2 Corinthians 10:4, 5; James 3:17, 18.

Forgiveness is in word and spirit – "*This is how my heavenly Father will treat each of you unless you forgive your brother from your heart*" Matthew 18:35 NIV; Psalm 49:7, 8; Ephesians 1:7; 2:8-9.

Sins passed through generations – Exodus 34:7; "*Watch out that no bitterness takes root among you, for as it springs up it causes deep trouble, hurting many in their spiritual lives*" Hebrews 12:15 TLB.

God's provision for removal of sin – "*And it shall come to pass in that day, that his burden shall be taken away from off thy shoulder, and his yoke from off thy neck, and the yoke shall be destroyed because of the anointing*" Isaiah 10:27; "*Not by might, nor by power, but by my spirit, saith the Lord of hosts*" Zechariah 4:6.

4. People who never fully experience the joy of the Lord in their sex lives: *(circle one) (page 79)*

   a. are normal

   b. may have unfinished business in their spirits

   c. can't change

C. Only women can be sexually abused. *(pages 80-81)* ___ True ___ False

1. Name two tendencies that may occur in men who were abused. *(page 81)*

   a. ______________________ b. ______________________

2. Only our own sins need to be released from our lives. *(page 83)*

   ___ True ___ False

3. The longer we hold on to sins, the more ______________________ will be done to our lives. *(page 83)*

For Further Study:

Be free – Ephesians 6:10-18; James 4:7; 1 Peter 5:6-10.
Joy is birthed out of sorrow – *"Ye shall be sorrowful, but your sorrow shall be turned into joy. A woman when she is in travail hath sorrow, because her hour is come: but as soon as she is delivered of the child, she remembereth no more the anguish, for joy that a man is born into the world"* John 16:20-21; Esther 9:22; Jeremiah 31:9-17; John 16:20. *"Weeping may endure for a night, but joy cometh in the morning ... Thou hast turned for me my mourning into dancing: thou hast put off my sackcloth, and girded me with gladness"* Psalm 30:5, 11; *"They that sow in tears shall reap in joy"* Psalm 126:5.
In order to know the peace that passes all understanding, every area of life must be completely yielded to the Spirit of God – Romans 8:6. Holding on to any sin will create confusion that will prevent experiencing God's peace – 1 Peter 3:11, 12.
"But exhort one another daily, while it is called Today; lest any of you be hardened through the deceitfulness of sin" Hebrews 3:13.

4. How are sins passed from one generation to the next? *(pages 83-84)*

____

D. The process of release includes which of the following: *(circle all that apply) (pages 84-86)*

1. choose to forgive
2. pay an offering to the church
3. receive the power of the Holy Spirit
4. by faith forgive the person
5. call the person on the phone
6. reject images, attitudes and the spirit of the sin
7. ask God for a fresh infilling of the Holy Spirit
8. ask God to show you whom else you need to forgive

For Further Study:

"Looking diligently lest any man fail of the grace of God; lest any root of bitterness springing up trouble you, and thereby many be defiled" Hebrews 12:15.
Sins passed through generations – Exodus 34:7
God's provision for removal of sins – *"As far as the east is from the west, so far hath he removed our transgressions from us"* Psalm 103:12. *"And when ye stand praying, forgive, if ye have aught against any: that your Father also which is in heaven may forgive you your trespasses"* Mark 11:25.
God forgives as we forgive others – James 2:13. Parable of the Unmerciful Servant – Matthew 18:21-35
"Be ye therefore merciful, as your Father also is merciful. Judge not, and ye shall not be judged: condemn not, and ye shall not be condemned; forgive, and ye shall be forgiven; Give, and it shall be given unto you; good measure, pressed down, and shaken together, and running over, shall men give into your bosom. For with the same measure that ye mete withal it shall be measured to you again" Luke 6:36-38.

II. Receiving the Glory of Virginity (Chapter 6)

A. Young people are pressured to lose their virginity early in life. *(page 89)*

___ True ___ False

1. Being a virgin makes you the person ______________________________

so that you can have a ______________________________

with the person He brings to you. *(page 89)*

2. Look up Isaiah 5:20 KJV. "*Woe unto them that call* ______________ *good and* ______________ *evil; that put* ______________ *for light, and light for* ______________*; that put bitter for* ______________*, and* ______________ *for bitter!*"

For Further Study:

Words are visible expressions of what is in the heart. "*A good man out of the good treasure of his heart bringeth forth that which is good; and an evil man out of the evil treasure of his heart bringeth forth that which is evil: for of the abundance of the heart his mouth speaketh*" Luke 6:45; Proverbs 10:20, 32.

"*They are waxen fat, they shine: yea, they overpass the deeds of the wicked: they judge not the cause, the cause of the fatherless, yet they prosper; and the right of the needy do they not judge. Shall I not visit for these things? saith the Lord: shall not my soul be avenged on such a nation as this?*" Jeremiah 5:28-29.

Finding healing in the ministry of Jesus – Psalm 34:18

The ministry of the Lord Jesus to the human heart completely heals the trauma of loneliness, failure and rejection – Luke 4:18.

B. Name some factors that drive young men and women toward sex. *(pages 91-93)*

1. ______________________________

2. ______________________________

3. ______________________________

4. ______________________________

C. God cares about you and can bring healing and restoration into every situation. *(page 95)*

___ True ___ False

1. Even though your physical virginity may never be regained, ______________________________

____

______________________________. *(page 95)*

For Further Study:

The Lord's healing, acceptance, power and grace give the believer the ability to face the world and its reality – *"Yea, though I walk through the valley of the shadow of death, I will fear no evil: for thou art with me: thy rod and thy staff they comfort me. Thou preparest a table before me in the presence of mine enemies: thou anointest my head with oil; my cup runneth over"* Psalm 23:4-5.

Jesus gives a peace, an inner stability that is a mystery to the world but a comfort to the believer. *"Peace I leave with you, my peace I give unto you: not as the world giveth, give I unto you. Let not your heart be troubled, neither let it be afraid"* John 14:27. Also, see Philippians 4:7.

Restoration of virginity – *"And I will restore to you the years that the locust has eaten, the cankerworm, and the caterpillar, and the palmerworm"* Joel 2:25.

2. Read: *"I beseech you therefore, brethren, by the mercies of God, that ye present your bodies a living sacrifice, holy, acceptable unto God, which is your reasonable service"* Romans 12:1.

   Do you believe there are any young men today who have the guts, a love for God in their hearts and enough of a desire to serve God that they will present their bodies to God? *(page 96)*

   ___ Yes ___ No

D. Check the habits that are important in your Christian development. *(pages 100-101)*

___ read the Bible and pray daily ___ praise God for what He's doing in me

___ renew and purify my mind ___ get up at 4:30 a.m.

___ change myself instantly ___ become free in expressing my true self

For Further Study:

"Likewise reckon ye also yourselves to be dead indeed unto sin, but alive unto God through Jesus Christ our Lord. Let not sin therefore reign in your mortal body, that ye should obey it in the lusts thereof. Neither yield ye your members as instruments of unrighteousness unto sin: but yield yourselves unto God, as those that are alive from the dead, and your members as instruments of righteousness" Romans 6:11-13; 1 Corinthians 10:31.
"This book of the law shall not depart out of my mouth; but thou shalt meditate therein day and night, that thou mayest observe to do according to all that is written therein: for then thou shalt make thy way prosperous, and then thou shalt have good success" Joshua 1:8.
"And be not conformed to this world: but be ye transformed by the renewing of your mind, that ye may prove what is that good, and acceptable, and perfect, will of God" Romans 12:2.

Practical:

Look up the following verses and comment on what they mean to you in light of these lessons.

1. Hebrews 12:15 ____________________
2. John 20:22-23 ____________________
3. Ephesians 4:32 ____________________
4. Jeremiah 32:18 ____________________
5. Psalm 138:8 ____________________
6. Isaiah 25:8 ____________________
7. Psalm 51:6-7 ____________________
8. Philippians 3:10-11 ____________________
9. Philippians 2:13 ____________________

For Further Study:

"Wherefore as the Holy Ghost saith Today if ye will hear his voice, Harden not your hearts, as in the provocation, in the day of temptation in the wilderness" Hebrews 3:7-8.

"Keeping mercy for thousands, forgiving iniquity and transgression and sin, and that will by no means clear the guilty; visiting the iniquity of the fathers upon the children, and upon the children's children, unto the third and to the fourth generation" Exodus 34:7.

"Looking unto Jesus the author and finisher of our faith; who for the joy that was set before him endured the cross, despising the shame, and is set down at the right hand of the throne of God" Hebrews 12:2.

"Being confident of this very thing, that he which hath begun a good work in you will perform it until the day of Jesus Christ" Philippians 1:6.

Read this prayer out loud for "release":

Father, in the Name of Jesus, I confess that You created me to be a man of God. You created me for a purpose and put within me everything I would need to accomplish it. I thank You for who You created me to be. I confess that all I ever want to be is that special person You created me to be. Now, by faith, I receive a fresh anointing of the Holy Spirit. And by the authority of Your Word in my life and the power of Your Spirit, I forgive ______________ who has made my life so miserable. I forgive him/her, Lord, with all my heart. Now, Father, I receive the righteousness and worthiness of Jesus Christ in my life. I am being changed from glory to glory, and I receive more of it right now. Thank You for it! Amen.

For Further Study:

Receive release – "*For the weapons of our warfare are not carnal, but mighty through God to the pulling down of strong holds; Casting down imaginations, and every high thing that exalteth itself against the knowledge of God, and bringing into captivity every thought to the obedience of Christ*" 2 Corinthians 10:4, 5; Luke 4:18.

Read this prayer out loud for "the glory of virginity":

Father, in the Name of Jesus, I'm coming to You right now because You've made me a man. I want to be a man of God in every area of my life—my mind, my heart, my spirit, my body. Please forgive me for every thought, word or action that has been sinful in my life. Thank You for forgiving me. Thank You, Lord, that I've been born into the Kingdom of God. I've been born into Your Spirit. I'm a partaker of Your Divine Nature through my Savior Jesus Christ. Satan has no rights to me. And by the authority of Your Word and the ability of Your Spirit, I rebuke the powers of darkness. I turn toward that spirit of lust, and say, "Spirit of lust, get out of my life in the Name of Jesus. I am receiving the glory of virginity, and I reject your lust." And now, Lord, by faith I receive the glory of virginity into my spirit. I present to You my body—holy, acceptable, which is my reasonable service. I not only present it to You, Lord, but by the power of Your Word and Your Spirit, I hold my body in the glory of virginity to present it to the woman I marry as the unique gift You gave me. I want my sex life to be pure, holy, righteous and good—the way You intended it to be. I don't want to sin. I don't want unrighteousness. I want the glory, Lord, in my life, in my marriage—I want it even if I never get married. I praise You for the glory of virginity right now. Thank You, Lord. Amen.

Principles I want to memorize:

Self Test *Lesson 5*

1. Past abuses in a person's life will normally cause no future problems. ___ True ___ False

2. Write out a definition of the "principle of release."

   ____

   ____

3. Release begins with a decision to ______________ the person who has hurt or harmed you.

4. Unforgiveness ______________________ the sins of others to us. *(circle one)*

   a. releases b. binds c. complicates

5. The effect of sin cannot be passed from generation to generation. ___ True ___ False

6. Remaining a virgin until marriage allows you to have a holy covenant relationship with your spouse.

   ___ True ___ False

7. Many men are unable to love or be loved normally because of lack of affection shown them in their own childhood. ___ True ___ False

8. God is a God of restoration and resurrection. **In your own words,** write out what is required to receive back into your life the "spirit and glory" of virginity.

   ____

   ____

   ____

   ____

Keep this test for your own records.

Lesson 6

Resisting Peer Pressure

Lesson 6
Resisting Peer Pressure

A. Name some of the problems young people face today. *(page 103)*

____

1. Check True or False for the following sentences: *(pages 104-105)*

___ True ___ False Loneliness is healthy and desirable.

___ True ___ False Friends are the antidote to loneliness.

___ True ___ False Initiation never leads to finding acceptance.

___ True ___ False Jesus will heal completely the trauma of loneliness and rejection.

___ True ___ False The Lord's ministry allows you to face the world and reality.

___ True ___ False You need not be yielded to the Holy Spirit to experience peace.

___ True ___ False Doing what your heart knows is wrong has no effect on you.

For Further Study:

Prayer leads to friendship with God. Friendship with God is life's greatest treasure – Psalm 25:14; Proverbs 3:32.
Being with God dispels loneliness – *"I desire no one on earth as much as you!"* Psalm 73:25, 26 TLB.
Loneliness is not the same as being alone – Example: The Lord Jesus Christ – Matthew 14:23.
Loneliness is never desirable – *"I looked on my right hand, and beheld, but there was no man that would know me: refuge failed me; no man cared for my soul"* Psalm 142:4.
The antidote to loneliness – *"Ointment and perfume rejoice the heart: so doth the sweetness of a man's friend by hearty counsel"* Proverbs 27:9. Friends are Heaven's riches – Proverbs 17:17.
Inner witness through the peace of God – *"And let the peace ... from the Christ rule (act as umpire continually) in your hearts"* Colossians 3:15 AMP; *"But you have received the Holy Spirit and he lives within you, in your hearts ... he teaches you all things, and he is the Truth"* 1 John 2:27 TLB.

2. Read: *"For if you live according to [the dictates of] the flesh, you will surely die. But if through the power of the [Holy] Spirit you are [habitually] putting to death (making extinct, deadening) the [evil] deeds prompted by the body, you shall [really and genuinely] live forever"* Romans 8:13 AMP.

3. Whatever you give into in life grows ______________________________, while what you

   ______________________ grows ______________________________. *(page 105)*

B. Read: *"But God is faithful [to His Word and to His compassionate nature], and He [can be trusted] not to let you be tempted and tried and assayed beyond your ability and strength of resistance and power to endure, but with the temptation He will [always] also provide the way out (the means of escape to a landing place), that you may be capable and strong and powerful to bear up under it patiently"* 1 Corinthians 10:13b AMP.

1. What is sometimes the best response to evil? *(page 106)*

   ____

For Further Study:

"Run from anything that gives you the evil thoughts that young men often have, but stay close to anything that makes you want to do right" 2 Timothy 2:22 TLB; *"What comes out of a man is what makes him 'unclean.' For from within, out of men's hearts, come evil thoughts, sexual immorality, theft, murder, adultery, greed, malice, deceit, lewdness, envy, slander, arrogance and folly. All these evils come from inside and make a man 'unclean'"* Mark 7:20-23 NIV.

"Watch and pray, that ye enter not into temptation: the spirit indeed is willing, but the flesh is weak" Matthew 26:41.

"And lead us not into temptation, but deliver us from evil" Matthew 6:13; *"For we wrestle not against flesh and blood, but against principalities, against powers, against the rulers of the darkness of this world, against spiritual wickedness in heavenly places"* Ephesians 6:12.

2. The man who professes to hate sin but has a lingering love for it will continue to be

   ______________________________. *(page 106)*

3. Saying ________ to a friend enables you to say ________ to your talent and intelligence. *(page 106)*

4. How did Jesus overcome temptation? *(page 107)*

   ____

5. After Jesus overcame temptation, He returned ______________________________

   ______________________________. *(page 107)*

6. Jesus memorized vast portions of Scripture that helped Him defeat Satan. *(page 107)*

   ___ True ___ False

7. Success is based on the ability to say ________. *(page 107)*

For Further Study:

"And when he had fasted forty days and forty nights, he was afterward an hungered. And when the tempter came to him, he said, If thou be the Son of God, command that these stones be made bread. But he answered and said, It is written, Man shall not live by bread alone, but by every word that proceedeth out of the mouth of God" Matthew 4:2-4.

"And when the devil had ended all the temptation, he departed from him for a season. And Jesus returned in the power of the Spirit into Galilee: and there went out a fame of him through all the region round about" Luke 4:13-14.

"Blessed is the man that walketh not in the counsel of the ungodly, nor standeth in the way of sinners, nor sitteth in the seat of the scornful" Psalm 1:1.

"For that they hated knowledge, and did not choose the fear of the Lord: They would none of my counsel: they despised all my reproof. Therefore shall they eat of the fruit of their own way, and be filled with their own devices" Proverbs 1:29-31.

C. Read Proverbs 1:10-15; 29-33, then answer the following based on the Scripture.

1. According to these verses, what are you to do if "sinners entice you"?

____

2. "Restrain your foot" means to do what in today's language?

____

3. Will those who try to tempt you get away with it? ______________

For Further Study:

The desire to belong represents one of the most basic needs of man – Genesis 2:18.
Rejection is one of life's cruelest blows – The Lord Jesus Christ *"came unto his own, and his own received him not"* John 1:11. Also, see Isaiah 53:3.
A feeling of rejection is often the root cause of suicide – Elijah – 1 Kings 19:4, 10.
Because of man's intense desire to be accepted and to belong, there is always pressure to go along with the gang – Proverbs 1:10, 15.
Fear – *"For God hath not given us the spirit of fear; but of power, and of love, and of a sound mind"* 2 Timothy 1:7; *"The wicked flee when no man pursueth: but the righteous are bold as a lion"* Proverbs 28:1; Genesis 3:10; Psalm 119:105; *"There is no fear in love; but perfect love casteth out fear: because fear hath torment"* 1 John 4:18.

D. What is at the root of peer pressure and the fear of man? *(page 109)*

____

____

1. The less you ____________ the more ____________ you gain. *(page 109)*
2. What happens when people overcome their fear of man? *(page 109)*

   ____

3. You find life by ____________ and by becoming identified with Jesus. *(page 110)*

For Further Study:

Moral cowardice causes men to shrink from duty and danger, to dread pain and to yield to fear – 1 Samuel 15:24.
The fear of man is a form of moral cowardice – Proverbs 29:25; Moral cowardice is the ruin of manhood – Numbers 13:33.
Boldness is a form of courage – Proverbs 18:10; Hebrews 13:6; 1 Peter 3:15; Successful men are bold in their identification with their belief, product or activity and in their confession of it – Psalm 119:46; Romans 1:16.
Overcome fear of men, openly identify with Jesus and be bold in confession of Him. *"And fear not them which kill the body, but are not able to kill the soul: but rather fear him which is able to destroy both soul and body in hell. Whosoever therefore shall confess me before men, him will I confess also before my Father which is in heaven"* Matthew 10:28, 32, 33.
"And they overcame him (the devil) by the blood of the Lamb, and by the word of their testimony; and they loved not their lives unto the death" Revelation 12:11.

E. Write the correct letter next to the sentense for the word that completes the sentence. *(pages 115-117)*

____ It is never too late to	a. date
____ If you do sin,	b. God
____ No sin is too great for God to	c. forgive
____ Satan can spoil your life only through *(choose 2)*	d. glory
____ If you can't date without sinning, don't	e. temptation
____ We are accepted as we are by	f. say "no"
____ Success is NOT based on the ability to	g. say "yes"
____ God desires your life to go from glory to	h. repent
	i. accusation

For Further Study:

"If we confess our sins, he is faithful and just to forgive us our sins, and to cleanse us from all unrighteousness" 1 John 1:9.

"And I heard a loud voice saying in heaven, Now is come salvation, and strength, and the kingdom of our God, and the power of his Christ: for the accuser of our brethren is cast down, which accused them before our God day and night" Revelation 12:10.

"Be sober, be vigilant; because your adversary the devil, as a roaring lion, walketh about, seeking whom he may devour" 1 Peter 5:8.

"There hath no temptation taken you but such as is common to man: but God is faithful, who will not suffer you to be tempted above that ye are able; but will with the temptation also make a way to escape, that ye may be able to bear it" 1 Corinthians 10:13.

"But we all, with open face beholding as in a glass the glory of the Lord, are changed into the same image from glory to glory, even as by the Spirit of the Lord" 2 Corinthians 3:18.

Practical:

1. How does Jesus deal with those who are wounded? Does He deal the same way with you?

   ____

2. Who most pressures you to sin?

   ____

   What can you do to resist pressure to sin?

   ____

For Further Study:

The power to resist wrong is the key to success. Jesus Christ overcame temptation with the Word of God – Luke 4:4, 8, 12. His submission to the Father, resistance to the devil and refusal to sin strengthened His spirit – Luke 4:14. To succeed in life as Jesus did, we must influence people to conform to our Godly standard of behavior – Romans 12:2.

Choices – *"I call heaven and earth to record this day against you, that I have set before you life and death, blessing and cursing: therefore choose life, that both thou and thy seed may live"* Deuteronomy 30:19. The freedom to choose between alternatives is the only true freedom in life – Galatians 5:13.

As Christians, we can choose to succeed or to fail; we can be wise or ignorant – Psalm 90:12. Our choices are shown by the company we keep – Proverbs 27:19 TLB.

3. A man finds himself in a car with a single woman to whom he is very attracted. She acts in an inviting way, and he struggles to resist temptation with her.

   What could he have done to "flee" evil?

   ____

   What can he do now?

   ____

For Further Study:

It takes courage to resist peer pressure and dare to be different – Psalm 119:51, 52; Daniel 1:8.
It takes courage to submit to righteousness – Psalm 119:30.
It takes courage to say "no" – *"I have refrained my feet from every evil way, that I might keep thy word"* Psalm 119:101.
It takes courage to admit a desire to be a man of God – *"Depart from me, ye evildoers: for I will keep the commandments of my God"* Psalm 119:115; *"Choosing rather to suffer affliction with the people of God, than to enjoy the pleasures of sin for a season"* Hebrews 11:25.

Repeat this prayer out loud:

Father, please give me the wisdom to walk in Your way and not follow others. Thank You for Your grace and forgiveness that covers all my sins and errors. Help me begin to see dangers before I am tempted to evil. And help me to love You with a pure heart all my days. Amen.

Principles I want to memorize:

Self Test *Lesson 6*

1. Loneliness is a normal, desirable way to live.

   ___ True ___ False

2. Complete this statement: Whatever you give into in life grows stronger, while ______________________________

   ____.

3. Sometimes the best response to evil is: *(circle one)*

   a. screaming

   b. standing up to it

   c. running away

4. Success is always based on the ability to say: *(circle one)*

   a. "yes" b. "no" c. "maybe"

5. How did Jesus overcome temptation?

   ____

   What was the result in His life?

   ____

   ____

6. You find your life by ____.

7. Satan can spoil your life only through ______________________________ or ______________________________.

Keep this test for your own records.

Final Exam

1. Decisions translate into energy.

   ___ True ___ False

2. Men are generally motivated by: *(circle one)*

   a. sports b. sound c. sight

3. What are the three most powerful words in the world? ______________________________

4. Men and women are to ______________________________ each other.

5. God has both feminine and masculine in Him.

   ___ True ___ False

6. Sex is the sign of the ______________________________.

7. Sex, circumcision and baptism are all ______________________________ signs of an ______________________________ work.

8. Living together is involvement. Getting married is:

   a. monotony b. consideration c. commitment

9. Love desires to benefit ______________________________.

   Lust desires to benefit ______________________________.

10. God made sex for ____________________ and giving, not for lusting and ____________________.

DETACH HERE

Final Exam

11. Briefly define fornication. ____

12. We cannot take portions of the Bible to justify our ________________. We must take our

    __________________________ and make them conform to ______________________________.

13. There is no such thing as a curse on men who slander women.

    ___ True ___ False

14. The comfort of the Holy Ghost in our lives is to be balanced with the ____________________

    _________________________.

15. With pornography, the image in the mind becomes an ____________________.

16. All sin promises to serve and to please, but actually ______________________________

    ____.

17. The greatest intimacy a man and woman will know comes from ______________________

    ______________________________.

18. The Kingdom of God is built on the positive; God will always end on the positive.

    ___ True ___ False

19. To renew your mind you must ____.

20. Past abuses not dealt with can normally be successfully covered up throughout life.

    ___ True ___ False

DETACH HERE

Final Exam

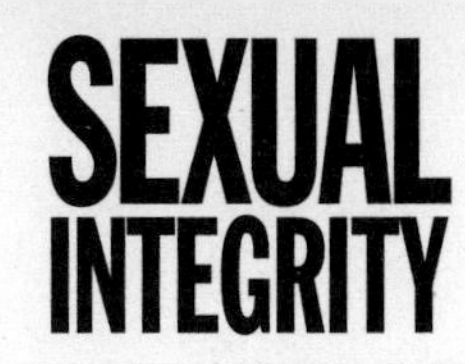

21. Write out a definition for the "principle of release."

____

____

22. What verses in the Bible have Jesus' principle of release? ______________________

–

23. The longer we hold on to sins, the more damage they will do to our lives. ___ True ___ False

24. How are sins passed from one generation to the next? ______________________

25. The Bible says, "*Woe unto them that call* ______________ *good and* ______________ *evil.*"

26. Being alone is often a good thing. Loneliness never is. ___ True ___ False

27. You must get rid of all known sin to experience true peace. ___ True ___ False

28. Whatever you give into in life grows ______________, while what you ______________ grows ______________________.

29. Running away is often the best response to evil. ___ True ___ False

30. Success is based ______________________________.

31. The fear of man is based on ______________________________

____.

32. Satan can spoil your life only through ______________________________ and ______________________.

DETACH HERE

33. Short essay: "Once an individual has lost his or her virginity, he or she is effectively doomed to live a life of despair. Nothing can be done, even with God, to change the situation."

Is this a valid statement or can something be done? Include steps to follow and Scriptures in your answer.

____

____

____

____

____

____

____

____

Name ____

Address ______________________ City ______________ State ____ Zip ________

Telephone a.m. ______________________ p.m. ______________________

Email Address ____

The Final Exam is required to be "commissioned."

For more information, contact
Christian Men's Network | P.O. Box 93478 | Southlake, TX 76092
ChristianMensNetwork.com | office@ChristianMensNetwork.com | 817-437-4888

Basic Daily Bible Reading

Read Proverbs each morning for wisdom, Psalms each evening for courage. Make copies of this chart and keep it in your Bible to mark off as you read. If you are just starting the habit of Bible reading, be aware that longer translations or paraphrases (such as Amplified and Living) will take longer to read each day. As you start, it is okay to read only one of the chapters in Psalms each night, instead of the many listed. Mark your chart so you'll remember which ones you haven't read.

NOTE: The chronological chart following has the rest of the chapters of Psalms that are not listed here. By using both charts together, you will cover the entire book of Psalms.

Day of Month	Proverbs	Psalms
1	1	1, 2, 4, 5, 6
2	2	7, 8, 9
3	3	10, 11, 12, 13, 14, 15
4	4	16, 17, 19, 20
5	5	21, 22, 23
6	6	24, 25, 26, 27
7	7	28, 29, 31, 32
8	8	33, 35
9	9	36, 37
10	10	38, 39, 40
11	11	41, 42, 43, 45, 46
12	12	47, 48, 49, 50
13	13	53, 55, 58, 61, 62
14	14	64, 65, 66, 67
15	15	68, 69
16	16	70, 71, 73
17	17	75, 76, 77, 81

Day of Month	Proverbs	Psalms
18	18	82, 83, 84, 85
19	19	87, 88, 91, 92
20	20	93, 94, 95, 97
21	21	98, 99, 100, 101, 103
22	22	104, 108
23	23	109, 110, 111
24	24	112, 113, 114, 115, 117
25	25	119:1-56
26	26	119:57-112
27	27	119:113-176
28	28	120, 121, 122, 124, 130, 131, 133, 134
29	29	135, 136, 138
30	30	139, 140, 141, 143
31	31	144, 145, 146, 148, 150

Chronological Annual Bible Reading

This schedule follows the events of the Bible chronologically and can be used with any translation or paraphrase of the Bible. Each day has an average of 77 verses of Scripture. If you follow this annually, along with your Daily Bible Reading, by your third year, you will recognize where you are and what is going to happen next. By your fifth year, you will understand the Scriptural background and setting for any reference spoken of in a message or book. At that point, the Word will become more like "meat" to you and less like "milk." Once you understand the basic stories and what happens on the surface, God can reveal to you the layers of meaning beneath. So, make copies of this chart to keep in your Bible and mark off as you read. And start reading—it's the greatest adventure in life!

Some notes:

1. Some modern translations don't have verses numbered (such as The Message), so they cannot be used with this chart. Also, if you are just starting the Bible, be aware that longer translations or paraphrases (such as Amplified and Living) tend to take longer to read each day.
2. The Daily Bible Reading chart covers the Proverbs and the chapters of Psalms that are not listed here. By using both charts together, you will cover the entire books of Psalms and Proverbs along with the rest of the Bible.
3. The chronology of Scripture is obvious in some cases, educated guesswork in others. The placement of Job, for example, is purely conjecture since there is no consensus among Bible scholars as to its date or place. For the most part, however, chronological reading helps the reader, since it places stories that have duplicated information, or prophetic utterances elsewhere in Scripture, within the same reading sequence.

HOW TO READ SCRIPTURE NOTATIONS:

Book chapter: verse. (Mark 15:44 means the book of Mark, chapter 15, verse 44.)

Book chapter; chapter (Mark 15; 16; 17 means the book of Mark, chapters 15, 16, 17.)

Books continue the same until otherwise noted. (2 Kings 22; 23:1-28; Jeremiah 20 means the book of 2 Kings, chapter 22, the book of
2 Kings, chapter 23, verses 1-28; then the book of Jeremiah, chapter 20.)

MAJORING IN MEN®

1	Jan 1	Genesis 1; 2; 3
2	Jan 2	Genesis 4; 5; 6
3	Jan 3	Genesis 7; 8; 9
4	Jan 4	Genesis 10; 11; 12
5	Jan 5	Genesis 13; 14; 15; 16
6	Jan 6	Genesis 17; 18; 19:1-29
7	Jan 7	Genesis 19:30-38; 20; 21
8	Jan 8	Genesis 22; 23; 24:1-31
9	Jan 9	Genesis 24:32-67; 25
10	Jan 10	Genesis 26; 27
11	Jan 11	Genesis 28; 29; 30:1-24
12	Jan 12	Genesis 30:25-43; 31
13	Jan 13	Genesis 32; 33; 34
14	Jan 14	Genesis 35; 36
15	Jan 15	Genesis 37; 38; 39
16	Jan 16	Genesis 40; 41
17	Jan 17	Genesis 42; 43
18	Jan 18	Genesis 44; 45
19	Jan 19	Genesis 46; 47; 48
20	Jan 20	Genesis 49; 50; Exodus 1
21	Jan 21	Exodus 2; 3; 4
22	Jan 22	Exodus 5; 6; 7
23	Jan 23	Exodus 8; 9
24	Jan 24	Exodus 10; 11; 12
25	Jan 25	Exodus 13; 14; 15
26	Jan 26	Exodus 16; 17; 18
27	Jan 27	Exodus 19; 20; 21
28	Jan 28	Exodus 22; 23; 24
29	Jan 29	Exodus 25; 26
30	Jan 30	Exodus 27; 28; 29:1-28
31	Jan 31	Exodus 29:29-46; 30; 31
32	Feb 1	Exodus 32; 33; 34
33	Feb 2	Exodus 35; 36
34	Feb 3	Exodus 37; 38
35	Feb 4	Exodus 39; 40
36	Feb 5	Leviticus 1; 2; 3; 4
37	Feb 6	Leviticus 5; 6; 7
38	Feb 7	Leviticus 8; 9; 10
39	Feb 8	Leviticus 11; 12; 13:1-37
40	Feb 9	Leviticus 13:38-59; 14
41	Feb 10	Leviticus 15; 16
42	Feb 11	Leviticus 17; 18; 19
43	Feb 12	Leviticus 20; 21; 22:1-16
44	Feb 13	Leviticus 22:17-33; 23
45	Feb 14	Leviticus 24; 25
46	Feb 15	Leviticus 26; 27
47	Feb 16	Numbers 1; 2
48	Feb 17	Numbers 3; 4:1-20
49	Feb 18	Numbers 4:21-49; 5; 6
50	Feb 19	Numbers 7
51	Feb 20	Numbers 8; 9; 10
52	Feb 21	Numbers 11; 12; 13
53	Feb 22	Numbers 14; 15
54	Feb 23	Numbers 16; 17
55	Feb 24	Numbers 18; 19; 20
56	Feb 25	Numbers 21; 22
57	Feb 26	Numbers 23; 24; 25
58	Feb 27	Numbers 26; 27
59	Feb 28	Numbers 28; 29; 30
60	Mar 1	Numbers 31, 32:1-27
61	Mar 2	Numbers 32:28-42; 33
62	Mar 3	Numbers 34; 35; 36
63	Mar 4	Deuteronomy 1; 2
64	Mar 5	Deuteronomy 3; 4
65	Mar 6	Deuteronomy 5; 6; 7
66	Mar 7	Deuteronomy 8; 9; 10
67	Mar 8	Deuteronomy 11; 12; 13
68	Mar 9	Deuteronomy 14; 15; 16
69	Mar 10	Deuteronomy 17; 18; 19; 20
70	Mar 11	Deuteronomy 21; 22; 23
71	Mar 12	Deuteronomy 24; 25; 26; 27
72	Mar 13	Deuteronomy 28
73	Mar 14	Deuteronomy 29; 30; 31
74	Mar 15	Deuteronomy 32; 33
75	Mar 16	Deuteronomy 34; Psalm 90; Joshua 1; 2
76	Mar 17	Joshua 3; 4; 5; 6
77	Mar 18	Joshua 7; 8; 9
78	Mar 19	Joshua 10; 11
79	Mar 20	Joshua 12; 13; 14
80	Mar 21	Joshua 15; 16
81	Mar 22	Joshua 17; 18; 19:1-23
82	Mar 23	Joshua 19:24-51; 20; 21
83	Mar 24	Joshua 22; 23; 24
84	Mar 25	Judges 1; 2; 3:1-11
85	Mar 26	Judges 3:12-31; 4; 5
86	Mar 27	Judges 6; 7
87	Mar 28	Judges 8; 9
88	Mar 29	Judges 10; 11; 12
89	Mar 30	Judges 13; 14; 15
90	Mar 31	Judges 16; 17; 18
91	Apr 1	Judges 19; 20

You have completed 1/4 of the Bible!

92	Apr 2	Judges 21; Job 1; 2; 3
93	Apr 3	Job 4; 5; 6
94	Apr 4	Job 7; 8; 9
95	Apr 5	Job 10; 11; 12
96	Apr 6	Job 13; 14; 15
97	Apr 7	Job 16; 17; 18; 19
98	Apr 8	Job 20; 21
99	Apr 9	Job 22; 23; 24
100	Apr 10	Job 25; 26; 27; 28
101	Apr 11	Job 29; 30; 31
102	Apr 12	Job 32; 33; 34
103	Apr 13	Job 35; 36; 37
104	Apr 14	Job 38; 39
105	Apr 15	Job 40; 41; 42
106	Apr 16	Ruth 1; 2; 3
107	Apr 17	Ruth 4; 1 Samuel 1; 2
108	Apr 18	1 Samuel 3; 4; 5; 6
109	Apr 19	1 Samuel 7; 8; 9
110	Apr 20	1 Samuel 10; 11; 12; 13
111	Apr 21	1 Samuel 14; 15
112	Apr 22	1 Samuel 16; 17
113	Apr 23	1 Samuel 18; 19; Psalm 59
114	Apr 24	1 Samuel 20; 21; Psalms 34; 56
115	Apr 25	1 Samuel 22; 23, Psalms 52; 142
116	Apr 26	1 Samuel 24; 25; 1 Chronicles 12:8-18; Psalm 57
117	Apr 27	1 Samuel 26; 27; 28; Psalms 54; 63
118	Apr 28	1 Samuel 29; 30; 31; 1 Chronicles 12:1-7; 12:19-22
119	Apr 29	1 Chronicles 10; 2 Samuel 1; 2
120	Apr 30	2 Samuel 3; 4; 1 Chronicles 11:1-9; 12:23-40
121	May 1	2 Samuel 5; 6; 1 Chronicles 13; 14
122	May 2	2 Samuel 22; 1 Chronicles 15
123	May 3	1 Chronicles 16; Psalm 18
124	May 4	2 Samuel 7; Psalms 96; 105
125	May 5	1 Chronicles 17; 2 Samuel 8; 9; 10
126	May 6	1 Chronicles 18; 19; Psalm 60; 2 Samuel 11
127	May 7	2 Samuel 12; 13; 1 Chronicles 20:1-3; Psalm 51
128	May 8	2 Samuel 14; 15
129	May 9	2 Samuel 16; 17; 18; Psalm 3
130	May 10	2 Samuel 19; 20; 21
131	May 11	2 Samuel 23:8-23
132	May 12	1 Chronicles 20:4-8; 11:10-25; 2 Samuel 23:24-39; 24
133	May 13	1 Chronicles 11:26-47; 21; 22
134	May 14	1 Chronicles 23; 24; Psalm 30
135	May 15	1 Chronicles 25; 26
136	May 16	1 Chronicles 27; 28; 29
137	May 17	1 Kings 1; 2:1-12; 2 Samuel 23:1-7
138	May 18	1 Kings 2:13-46; 3; 2 Chronicles 1:1-13
139	May 19	1 Kings 5; 6; 2 Chronicles 2
140	May 20	1 Kings 7; 2 Chronicles 3; 4
141	May 21	1 Kings 8; 2 Chronicles 5
142	May 22	1 Kings 9; 2 Chronicles 6; 7:1-10
143	May 23	1 Kings 10:1-13; 2 Chronicles 7:11-22; 8; 9:1-12; 1 Kings 4
144	May 24	1 Kings 10:14-29; 2 Chronicles 1:14-17; 9:13-28; Psalms 72; 127
145	May 25	Song of Solomon 1; 2; 3; 4; 5
146	May 26	Song of Solomon 6; 7; 8; 1 Kings 11:1-40
147	May 27	Ecclesiastes 1; 2; 3; 4
148	May 28	Ecclesiastes 5; 6; 7; 8
149	May 29	Ecclesiastes 9; 10; 11; 12; 1 Kings 11:41-43; 2 Chronicles 9:29-31
150	May 30	1 Kings 12; 2 Chronicles 10; 11
151	May 31	1 Kings 13; 14; 2 Chronicles 12
152	June 1	1 Kings 15; 2 Chronicles 13; 14; 15
153	June 2	1 Kings 16; 2 Chronicles 16; 17
154	June 3	1 Kings 17; 18; 19
155	June 4	1 Kings 20; 21
156	June 5	1 Kings 22; 2 Chronicles 18
157	June 6	2 Kings 1; 2; 2 Chronicles 19; 20; 21:1-3
158	June 7	2 Kings 3; 4
159	June 8	2 Kings 5; 6; 7
160	June 9	2 Kings 8; 9; 2 Chronicles 21:4-20

MAJORING IN MEN®

161	June 10	2 Chronicles 22; 23; 2 Kings 10; 11
162	June 11	Joel 1; 2; 3
163	June 12	2 Kings 12; 13; 2 Chronicles 24
164	June 13	2 Kings 14; 2 Chronicles 25; Jonah 1
165	June 14	Jonah 2; 3; 4; Hosea 1; 2; 3; 4
166	June 15	Hosea 5; 6; 7; 8; 9; 10
167	June 16	Hosea 11; 12; 13; 14
168	June 17	2 Kings 15:1-7; 2 Chronicles 26; Amos 1; 2; 3
169	June 18	Amos 4; 5; 6; 7
170	June 19	Amos 8; 9; 2 Kings 15:8-18; Isaiah 1
171	June 20	Isaiah 2; 3; 4; 2 Kings 15:19-38; 2 Chronicles 27
172	June 21	Isaiah 5; 6; Micah 1; 2; 3
173	June 22	Micah 4; 5; 6; 7; 2 Kings 16:1-18
174	June 23	2 Chronicles 28; Isaiah 7; 8
175	June 24	Isaiah 9; 10; 11; 12
176	June 25	Isaiah 13; 14; 15; 16
177	June 26	Isaiah 17; 18; 19; 20; 21
178	June 27	Isaiah 22; 23; 24; 25
179	June 28	Isaiah 26; 27; 28; 29
180	June 29	Isaiah 30; 31; 32; 33
181	June 30	Isaiah 34; 35; 2 Kings 18:1-8; 2 Chronicles 29
182	July 1	2 Chronicles 30; 31; 2 Kings 17; 2 Kings 16:19-20

You have completed 1/2 of the Bible!

183	July 2	2 Kings 18:9-37; 2 Chronicles 32:1-19; Isaiah 36
184	July 3	2 Kings 19; 2 Chronicles 32:20-23; Isaiah 37
185	July 4	2 Kings 20; 21:1-18; 2 Chronicles 32:24-33; Isaiah 38; 39
186	July 5	2 Chronicles 33:1-20; Isaiah 40; 41
187	July 6	Isaiah 42; 43; 44
188	July 7	Isaiah 45; 46; 47; 48
189	July 8	Isaiah 49; 50; 51; 52
190	July 9	Isaiah 53; 54; 55; 56; 57
191	July 10	Isaiah 58; 59; 60; 61; 62
192	July 11	Isaiah 63; 64; 65; 66
193	July 12	2 Kings 21:19-26; 2 Chronicles 33:21-25; 34:1-7; Zephaniah 1; 2; 3
194	July 13	Jeremiah 1; 2; 3
195	July 14	Jeremiah 4; 5
196	July 15	Jeremiah 6; 7; 8
197	July 16	Jeremiah 9; 10; 11
198	July 17	Jeremiah 12; 13; 14; 15
199	July 18	Jeremiah 16; 17; 18; 19
200	July 19	Jeremiah 20; 2 Kings 22; 23:1-28
201	July 20	2 Chronicles 34:8-33; 35:1-19; Nahum 1; 2; 3
202	July 21	2 Kings 23:29-37; 2 Chronicles 35:20-27; 36:1-5; Jeremiah 22:10-17; 26; Habakkuk 1
203	July 22	Habakkuk 2; 3; Jeremiah 46; 47; 2 Kings 24:1-4; 2 Chronicles 36:6-7
204	July 23	Jeremiah 25; 35; 36; 45
205	July 24	Jeremiah 48; 49:1-33
206	July 25	Daniel 1; 2
207	July 26	Jeremiah 22:18-30; 2 Kings 24:5-20; 2 Chronicles 36:8-12; Jeremiah 37:1-2; 52:1-3; 24; 29
208	July 27	Jeremiah 27; 28; 23
209	July 28	Jeremiah 50; 51:1-19
210	July 29	Jeremiah 51:20-64; 49:34-39; 34
211	July 30	Ezekiel 1; 2; 3; 4
212	July 31	Ezekiel 5; 6; 7; 8
213	Aug 1	Ezekiel 9; 10; 11; 12
214	Aug 2	Ezekiel 13, 14, 15, 16:1-34
215	Aug 3	Ezekiel 16:35-63; 17; 18
216	Aug 4	Ezekiel 19; 20
217	Aug 5	Ezekiel 21; 22
218	Aug 6	Ezekiel 23; 2 Kings 25:1; 2 Chronicles 36:13-16; Jeremiah 39:1; 52:4; Ezekiel 24
219	Aug 7	Jeremiah 21; 22:1-9; 32; 30
220	Aug 8	Jeremiah 31; 33; Ezekiel 25
221	Aug 9	Ezekiel 29:1-16; 30; 31; 26
222	Aug 10	Ezekiel 27; 28; Jeremiah 37:3-21
223	Aug 11	Jeremiah 38; 39:2-10; 52:5-30
224	Aug 12	2 Kings 25:2-22; 2 Chronicles 36:17-21; Jeremiah 39:11-18; 40:1-6; Lamentations 1
225	Aug 13	Lamentations 2; 3
226	Aug 14	Lamentations 4; 5; Obadiah; Jeremiah 40:7-16
227	Aug 15	Jeremiah 41; 42; 43; 44; 2 Kings 25:23-26
228	Aug 16	Ezekiel 33:21-33; 34; 35; 36
229	Aug 17	Ezekiel 37; 38; 39
230	Aug 18	Ezekiel 32; 33:1-20; Daniel 3
231	Aug 19	Ezekiel 40; 41
232	Aug 20	Ezekiel 42; 43; 44
233	Aug 21	Ezekiel 45; 46; 47
234	Aug 22	Ezekiel 48; 29:17-21; Daniel 4
235	Aug 23	Jeremiah 52:31-34; 2 Kings 25:27-30; Psalms 44; 74; 79
236	Aug 24	Psalms 80; 86; 89
237	Aug 25	Psalms 102; 106
238	Aug 26	Psalms 123; 137; Daniel 7; 8
239	Aug 27	Daniel 5; 9; 6
240	Aug 28	2 Chronicles 36:22-23; Ezra 1; 2
241	Aug 29	Ezra 3; 4:1-5; Daniel 10; 11
242	Aug 30	Daniel 12; Ezra 4:6-24; 5; 6:1-13; Haggai 1
243	Aug 31	Haggai 2; Zechariah 1; 2; 3
244	Sept 1	Zechariah 4; 5; 6; 7; 8
245	Sept 2	Ezra 6:14-22; Psalm 78
246	Sept 3	Psalms 107; 116; 118
247	Sept 4	Psalms 125; 126; 128; 129; 132; 147
248	Sept 5	Psalm 149; Zechariah 9; 10; 11; 12; 13
249	Sept 6	Zechariah 14; Esther 1; 2; 3
250	Sept 7	Esther 4; 5; 6; 7; 8
251	Sept 8	Esther 9; 10; Ezra 7; 8
252	Sept 9	Ezra 9; 10; Nehemiah 1
253	Sept 10	Nehemiah 2; 3; 4; 5
254	Sept 11	Nehemiah 6; 7
255	Sept 12	Nehemiah 8; 9; 10
256	Sept 13	Nehemiah 11; 12
257	Sept 14	Nehemiah 13; Malachi 1; 2; 3; 4
258	Sept 15	1 Chronicles 1; 2:1-35
259	Sept 16	1 Chronicles 2:36-55; 3; 4
260	Sept 17	1 Chronicles 5; 6:1-41
261	Sept 18	1 Chronicles 6:42-81; 7
262	Sept 19	1 Chronicles 8; 9
263	Sept 20	Matthew 1; 2; 3; 4
264	Sept 21	Matthew 5; 6
265	Sept 22	Matthew 7; 8
266	Sept 23	Matthew 9; 10
267	Sept 24	Matthew 11; 12
268	Sept 25	Matthew 13; 14
269	Sept 26	Matthew 15; 16
270	Sept 27	Matthew 17; 18; 19
271	Sept 28	Matthew 20; 21
272	Sept 29	Matthew 22; 23
273	Sept 30	Matthew 24; 25

You have completed 3/4 of the Bible!

274	Oct 1	Matthew 26; 27; 28
275	Oct 2	Mark 1; 2
276	Oct 3	Mark 3; 4
277	Oct 4	Mark 5; 6
278	Oct 5	Mark 7; 8:1-26
279	Oct 6	Mark 8:27-38; 9
280	Oct 7	Mark 10; 11
281	Oct 8	Mark 12; 13
282	Oct 9	Mark 14
283	Oct 10	Mark 15; 16
284	Oct 11	Luke 1
285	Oct 12	Luke 2; 3
286	Oct 13	Luke 4; 5
287	Oct 14	Luke 6; 7:1-23
288	Oct 15	Luke 7:24-50; 8
289	Oct 16	Luke 9
290	Oct 17	Luke 10; 11
291	Oct 18	Luke 12; 13
292	Oct 19	Luke 14; 15
293	Oct 20	Luke 16; 17
294	Oct 21	Luke 18; 19
295	Oct 22	Luke 20; 21
296	Oct 23	Luke 22
297	Oct 24	Luke 23; 24:1-28
298	Oct 25	Luke 24:29-53; John 1
299	Oct 26	John 2; 3; 4:1-23
300	Oct 27	John 4:24-54; 5; 6:1-7
301	Oct 28	John 6:8-71; 7:1-21
302	Oct 29	John 7:22-53; 8
303	Oct 30	John 9; 10
304	Oct 31	John 11; 12:1-28
305	Nov 1	John 12:29-50; 13; 14
306	Nov 2	John 15; 16; 17
307	Nov 3	John 18; 19:1-24

MAJORING IN MEN®

Day	Date	Reading
308	Nov 4	John 19:25-42; 20; 21
309	Nov 5	Acts 1; 2
310	Nov 6	Acts 3; 4
311	Nov 7	Acts 5; 6
312	Nov 8	Acts 7
313	Nov 9	Acts 8; 9
314	Nov 10	Acts 10
315	Nov 11	Acts 11
316	Nov 12	Acts 12; 13
317	Nov 13	Acts 14; 15; Galatians 1
318	Nov 14	Galatians 2; 3; 4
319	Nov 15	Galatians 5; 6; James 1
320	Nov 16	James 2; 3; 4; 5
321	Nov 17	Acts 16; 17
322	Nov 18	Acts 18:1-11; 1 Thessalonians 1; 2; 3; 4
323	Nov 19	1 Thessalonians 5; 2 Thessalonians 1; 2; 3
324	Nov 20	Acts 18:12-28; 19:1-22; 1 Corinthians 1
325	Nov 21	1 Corinthians 2; 3; 4; 5
326	Nov 22	1 Corinthians 6; 7; 8
327	Nov 23	1 Corinthians 9; 10; 11
328	Nov 24	1 Corinthians 12; 13; 14
329	Nov 25	1 Corinthians 15; 16
330	Nov 26	Acts 19:23-41; 20:1; 2 Corinthians 1; 2
331	Nov 27	2 Corinthians 3; 4; 5
332	Nov 28	2 Corinthians 6; 7; 8; 9
333	Nov 29	2 Corinthians 10; 11; 12
334	Nov 30	2 Corinthians 13; Romans 1; 2
335	Dec 1	Romans 3; 4; 5
336	Dec 2	Romans 6; 7; 8
337	Dec 3	Romans 9; 10; 11
338	Dec 4	Romans 12; 13; 14
339	Dec 5	Romans 15; 16
340	Dec 6	Acts 20:2-38; 21
341	Dec 7	Acts 22; 23
342	Dec 8	Acts 24; 25; 26
343	Dec 9	Acts 27; 28
344	Dec 10	Ephesians 1; 2; 3
345	Dec 11	Ephesians 4; 5; 6
346	Dec 12	Colossians 1; 2; 3
347	Dec 13	Colossians 4; Philippians 1; 2
348	Dec 14	Philippians 3; 4; Philemon
349	Dec 15	1 Timothy 1; 2; 3; 4
350	Dec 16	1 Timothy 5; 6; Titus 1; 2
351	Dec 17	Titus 3; 2 Timothy 1; 2; 3
352	Dec 18	2 Timothy 4; 1 Peter 1; 2
353	Dec 19	1 Peter 3; 4; 5; Jude
354	Dec 20	2 Peter 1; 2; 3; Hebrews 1
355	Dec 21	Hebrews 2; 3; 4; 5
356	Dec 22	Hebrews 6; 7; 8; 9
357	Dec 23	Hebrews 10; 11
358	Dec 24	Hebrews 12; 13; 2 John; 3 John
359	Dec 25	1 John 1; 2; 3; 4
360	Dec 26	1 John 5; Revelation 1; 2
361	Dec 27	Revelation 3; 4; 5; 6
362	Dec 28	Revelation 7; 8; 9; 10; 11
363	Dec 29	Revelation 12; 13; 14; 15
364	Dec 30	Revelation 16; 17; 18; 19
365	Dec 31	Revelation 20; 21; 22

You have completed the entire Bible-Congratulations!

MAJORING IN MEN® CURRICULUM

MANHOOD GROWTH PLAN

Order the corresponding workbook for each book, and study the first four Majoring In Men® Curriculum books in this order:

MAXIMIZED MANHOOD: Realize your need for God in every area of your life and start mending relationships with Christ and your family.

COURAGE: Make peace with your past, learn the power of forgiveness and the value of character. Let yourself be challenged to speak up for Christ to other men.

COMMUNICATION, SEX AND MONEY: Increase your ability to communicate, place the right values on sex and money in relationships, and greatly improve relationships, whether married or single.

STRONG MEN IN TOUGH TIMES: Reframe trials, battles and discouragement in light of Scripture and gain solid footing for business, career, and relational choices in the future.

Choose five of the following books to study next. When you have completed nine books, if you are not in men's group, you can find a Majoring In Men® group near you and become "commissioned" to minister to other men.

DARING: Overcome fear to live a life of daring ambition for Godly pursuits.

SEXUAL INTEGRITY: Recognize the sacredness of the sexual union, overcome mistakes and blunders and commit to righteousness in your sexuality.

UNIQUE WOMAN: Discover what makes a woman tick, from adolescence through maturity, to be able to minister to a spouse's uniqueness at any age.

NEVER QUIT: Take the ten steps for entering or leaving any situation, job, relationship or crisis in life.

REAL MAN: Discover the deepest meaning of Christlikeness and learn to exercise good character in times of stress, success or failure.

POWER OF POTENTIAL: Start making solid business and career choices based on Biblical principles while building core character that affects your entire life.

ABSOLUTE ANSWERS: Adopt practical habits and pursue Biblical solutions to overcome "prodigal problems" and secret sins that hinder both success and satisfaction with life.

TREASURE: Practice Biblical solutions and principles on the job to find treasures such as the satisfaction of exercising integrity and a job well done.

IRRESISTIBLE HUSBAND: Avoid common mistakes that sabotage a relationship and learn simple solutions and good habits to build a marriage that will consistently increase in intensity for decades.

MAJORING IN MEN® CURRICULUM

CHURCH GROWTH PLAN

STRONG - SUSTAINABLE - SYNERGISTIC

THREE PRACTICAL PHASES TO A POWERFUL MEN'S MOVEMENT IN YOUR CHURCH

Phase One:

- Pastor disciples key men/men's director using Maximized Manhood system.
- Launch creates momentum among men
- Church becomes more attractive to hold men who visit
- Families grow stronger
- Men increase bond to pastor

Phase Two:

- Men/men's director teach other men within the church
- Increased tithing and giving by men
- Decreased number of families in crisis
- Increased mentoring of teens and children
- Increase of male volunteers
- Faster assimilation for men visitors - clear path for pastor to connect with new men
- Men pray regularly for pastor

Phase Three:

- Men teach other men outside the church and bring them to Christ
- Increased male population and attraction to a visiting man, seeing a place he belongs
- Stronger, better-attended community outreaches
- Men are loyal to and support pastor

This system enables the pastor to successfully train key leaders, create momentum, build a church that attracts and holds men who visit, and disciple strong men.

Churches may conduct men's ministry entirely free of charge! Learn how by calling 817-437-4888.

CONTACT
MAJORING IN MEN® CURRICULUM
817-437-4888
admin@ChristianMensNetwork.com

Christian Men's Network
P.O. Box 93478
Southlake, TX 76092

Great discounts available.

Start your discipleship TODAY!

Call today for group discounts
and coaching opportunities.

FREE DVD!
Send your name and address to:
office@ChristianMensNetwork.com
We'll send you a FREE full-length DVD
with ministry for men.
(Limit one per person.)

ABOUT THE AUTHOR

Edwin Louis Cole mentored hundreds of thousands of people through challenging events and powerful books that have become the most widely-used Christian men's resources in the world. He is known for pithy statements and a confrontational style that demanded social responsibility and family leadership.

After serving as a pastor, evangelist, and Christian television pioneer, and at an age when most men were retiring, he followed his greatest passion—to lead men into Christlikeness, which he called "real manhood."

Ed Cole was a real man through and through. A loving son to earthly parents and the heavenly Father. Devoted husband to the "loveliest lady in the land," Nancy Corbett Cole. Dedicated father to three and, over the years, accepting the role of "father" to thousands. A reader, a thinker, a visionary. A man who made mistakes, learned lessons, then shared the wealth of his wisdom with men around the world. The Christian Men's Network he founded in 1977 is still a vibrant, global ministry. Unquestionably, he was the greatest men's minister of his generation.

Facebook.com/EdwinLouisCole